CW01651994

AKRO
POLIS

Christmas in Bohemia

Traditional Czech Christmas cuisine and customs

Kamila Skopová

© Text and Illustration Kamila Skopová, 2004, 2012
© Translation Melvyn Clarke, 2012
© Filip Tomáš - Akropolis, 2012
ISBN 978-80-7470-015-6

CHRISTMAS

The very word Christmas evokes a great many feelings – memories of childhood, the smell of Mum's kitchen with all those traditional treats, vanilla crescents and fried carp – a home redolent with pine needles, burning candles and love. Lord knows just how much all that magical fragrance, conviviality, gratitude, faith and hope was needed (both from the children for a bountiful display of presents, and from the adults wishing for everything to be well again in the coming year) for the most wonderful festival of the year to crystallize over the centuries into Christmas – the Czech Christmas. For the Czech Christmas has its unique, exclusive place in the context of European and worldwide celebrations of the birth of Christ. It is Christian, but at the same time it has all the charm of folk bluntness, humour, superstitious magic and fortune-telling, passed down over the centuries from pagan times to the not so remote past. This spiritual wealth has come down to us along with the many little material artifacts that make up the Czech Christmas atmosphere, especially the unique creche scenes, from large-scale moving models down to a few tiny figures set in moss in a rural cottage window. Numerous other little works of art are also to be seen – braids (*vrkoče*), worlds (*světy*), hedgehogs (*ježci*), quiver trees (*třesolky*), sun orbs (*polazy*), carolling sticks (*koledni pruty*) and the like, which we admire to this day and occasionally try to revive, but for the most part we no longer know anything of the function of these folk-custom artifacts or the meaning that our ancestors ascribed to them.

Let us also recall the important individual feast days of Advent. November 30th is the Feast of St. Andrew, patron saint of lovers and engaged couples, when young people sought to have their futures told, particularly regarding love and future marriage. The Feast of Barbara on December 4th is marked by cherry branches, but it also used to involve mysterious white figures with hair falling loosely over their faces – little Barbaras, who made rounds visiting homes to reprimand or give presents to children. All the figures that make Advent rounds have the task of dealing out both punishments and presents, not only the well-known Bishop Nicholas with his angel and devils, but also St Ambrose on December 7th, and Lucka on the Feast of St Lucy the Light-bearer (though the weather lore: "Lucy sips at the night, but adds nothing to the day" only used to apply until the Julian calendar was changed to the Gregorian in 1582, with the loss of ten days, so the Feast of St Lucy no longer falls on the winter solstice). However, along with these more or less dignified saintly figures, some far more questionable "masked monsters" used to run around the Czech countryside during the Advent season, which very much bothered the church. But the mischief-and-humour-loving Czechs would not allow them to be banned, these

"naggikins", "horsikins", "goatikins", "motherkins" and the dreadful Perchta white ladies. But the Nicholas procession in the Litomyšl area, as described by Professor Čeněk Zíbrt, was almost identical to the Shrovetide processions, and only the dignified figure of Nicholas at the front beside the *Laufr* figure indicated that this was actually Nicholas's festive procession.

But above all, people looked forward to Christmas. They sang songs about the coming of the Saviour and prepared their homes for celebrations of his birth. Then as now they used to do the house-cleaning at this time. The entire workload of cleaning and meal preparation fell to the woman of the house, though the cottager in the mountains sometimes had a hard time of it too, as we know from the famous carol from the foothills of the Giant Mountains, in which he wandered around the middle of nowhere for all the required ingredients, only to be spanked with a shovel for bringing spoilt (obviously frozen solid) yeast and rock-hard cakes.

Perhaps the traditional food that varied most from place to place was that prepared at Christmas time: fruit sauce (*muzika, odvárka*), St Thomas preserve (*tomáškový kompot*), feather beds and oven loafers (*peřinky, peciválky*), Christmas cake (*štědrovka, houska, húsce, calta, vánočka*), millet gruel (*jahelník*), mushroom and barley casserole (*Černý Kuba*), fried peas (*pučálka*), honey gruel (*sladká kaše s medem*), mushroom soup and fish, both real and baked from dough.

Nowadays it is more likely to be traditional fish soup, fried carp and potato salad; in some places they maintain the tradition of grilled wine sausages (*opékané vinné klobásy*) (best grilled when wound up in spirals, skewered crosswise and covered in flour or breadcrumbs like a schnitzel). In a nutshell, "Christmas comes but once a year", so everyone indulges as health and purse permit. Of course, nowadays Christmas has been somewhat distorted by excessive commercialization. From October we are accompanied everywhere, even in quite inappropriate places, by carols and tawdry mass-produced tinsel. At home, too, we make very sure that we have enough food, drink and presents bought in, but somehow neglect the spiritual basis for celebrating such festivals. In times gone by, people mostly experienced privations and hard everyday work out of necessity, or sometimes even voluntarily. But when the time then came for festivities, they could really savour and relish them. Nowadays this healthy contrast is lacking – we live with a relative sufficiency of food and entertainment every day, which is to our detriment. It would do no harm at least during the Christmas season to return to the humility of our ancestors, and at least during the Christmas Eve supper to thank God, nature and people of goodwill for all the gifts that we can enjoy. And then to sing together and to celebrate the festival of the birth of our Lord among plenty, but in the knowledge that this plenty is not to be taken for granted.

In days gone by, the table, once a sacrosanct place in the household, was also ceremoniously set for the Christmas feast – one way for families living in the town and another way in the countryside. A white canvas sheet was spread across the table and hay was strewn underneath to ensure that enough of it was gathered the following year. The table legs had a chain wound around them in the hope that this would bind the family together throughout the coming year. On the table they placed everything that they hoped to have in abundance the following year – baked goods made out of white and rye flour, Christmas cake and bread, garlic against illnesses and the powers of evil, honey for the good of the heart, dried fruit, mushrooms and nuts, all meant to ensure fertility and abundance, as were peas and other pulses. On the table there were also ears of every type of grain and several small coins for good luck. Christmas Eve was always wreathed in a special mystique – it was an evening of fortune-telling and divination over the next harvest and family members' life and health. And even today, we of the computer generation are still a little apprehensive about whether or not the apple will be cut open to reveal a smiling star or a worm, or heaven forbid, a cross! And the whole world narrows down to the stretch of water in the container on which our nutshell boats sail, as we follow the path of our own like children with bated breath.

So may the little boat of your life always float on happy waters...

RECIPES

Christmas cake (Vánočka) 11

How is yeast dough prepared?

Above all with love, but then prepare all food that way and you shall be rewarded. You have to treat yeast dough just like a baby with a new nappy - tenderly, gently... and quickly!

Prepare the flour. This should be at room temperature and it is well worth passing it through a finer sieve. That way the flour is aerated, it rises better and any impurities are caught.

Mix the loose ingredients into the flour - the icing sugar, salt, vanilla, lemon peel and if possible ground aniseed and fennel (to prevent flatulence and to scent the dough). Crumble yeast into a cup, add a tablespoon of sugar, mix and pour over with warm milk. Add a handful of flour and divide the sourdough, which is left to rise in a warm place. Meanwhile prepare the egg yolks and heat the required amount of fat. Mix the sourdough, hot fat, egg yolks, rum and warm milk (as required - be careful not to "drown the miller"!) into the flour and with a stirrer or a cooking spoon knead until the dough is shiny and no longer sticks to the spoon. Then take out the cooking spoon, sprinkle the dough with flour, cover it in a teacloth and let it rise in a warm place. Harder dough, e.g.

for Christmas cake, should be worked over one more time by hand on a pastry board. Add raisins during this final work-over.

After the dough has been shaped out, leave it to finish rising on a heated, greased tray. Before baking, brush with whisked egg yolks and/or sprinkle with almonds and place in a well-heated but not a fierce oven. Do not open the oven for the first ten minutes. After it has been baked, carefully remove the tray with the cake, leave it to cool for a while and then carefully place it on the pastry board.

Housewives used to place their baking, e.g. Kermis cake, on clean rye straw, to allow it to "exhale" properly.

Baking a nice Christmas cake is not so complicated, but every year we have the same repeating dilemma: should the Christmas cake be nice and rich (but then it rarely keeps its shape), or should we cheat a little, but then its taste is not quite right, even if it is perfectly proportioned.

Cut the well-risen dough into eight pieces by halving it several times and then cut the eighth piece of dough in half again. Weave the "braid" from four strands, starting from the middle. Place the braid on a greased tray or, even better, on greased kitchen foil or baking paper spread out on the tray. With the back of your hand make a lengthwise hollow in the braid, pour in peeled and sliced roasted almonds and cover with the three-stranded tail,

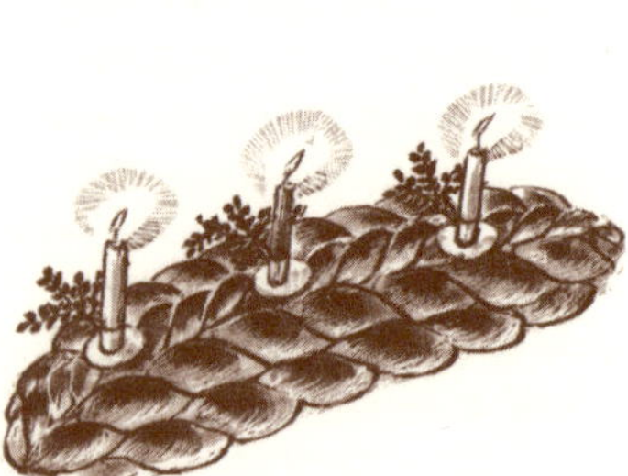

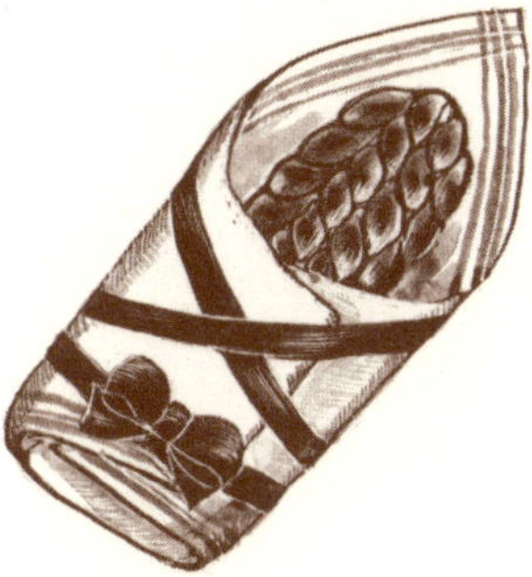

which is to be wound underneath from both sides. Again make a hollow, pour in the almonds and from the last eighth part of the dough that was halved, wind two strands round to crown the work. Again wind these two strands beneath the braid and leave the Christmas cake to rise. Then glaze with egg yolks, pour in more sliced almonds and bake. After baking for around fifteen minutes, lightly cover the Christmas cake in kitchen foil and finish baking. Before baking, it is a good idea to secure the shape of the braid with three skewers inserted diagonally through the body of the Christmas cake. You will find out if the risen dough is baked all the way through by carefully piercing it with a sharpened skewer. When you pull the skewer out, if it is still dry then the cake is ready. If the dough inside is not yet baked then it will adhere to the skewer, which will be sticky on the surface. Leave the baked Christmas cake to cool for a short while and then very carefully place it on the pastry board or on some other clean board that has not been used for other purposes. You may then sprinkle sugar over the cooled cake or decorate it in some other way.

The basic rule is that the more flour there is in the cake, the longer you bake it, i.e. a half kilo Christmas cake is baked for half an hour, a one-kilo cake is baked for about one hour and so on.

Christmas cake - dough recipe

750 g medium ground flour
150 g fat
150 g sugar
3 egg yolks, 1 egg yolk for glazing
1 tsp salt

vanilla sugar
spices (ground aniseed and fennel: approx 1 tsp)
lemon peel grated from a small well-washed lemon
a pinch of turmeric for colour
70 g yeast
warm milk as required
2 tbsps rum
raisins, peeled roasted almonds

Gingerbread (Perník)

The smell of gingerbread with pine, vanilla and burning candles is without doubt all part of the Christmas atmosphere. Gingerbread has been made in Bohemia since the early 14th century, when local cake makers used to bake it. Indeed they left a memorial of themselves in Prague, nowadays called Celetná Street (from *caletník* - cake maker). However, gingerbread in those days was different to the painted kind that we have today. Thick dough was stamped or "printed" in ornately carved molds made of hardwood from fruit trees and sprinkled with fine peasemeal, which gave the gingerbread baking in the oven a marvellous browny-red hue. To make the gingerbread shine the master gingerbread makers glazed it with cherry size. The dough was also prepared

differently. The first dough, the flour, honey and dark syrup with spices were processed and left to rise in wooden chests in the cellar for several years – some sources even say for several decades. The hardened dough was then separated with an axe. Again it had to be arduously reworked and mixed with other ingredients. Family recipes were kept strictly secret. Entirely in keeping with medieval tastes, pepper (in Latin *piper*) was added to the dough, from which the gingerbread makers acquired the grand title of "artopiperists". The original Czech name for gingerbread was from pepper – *peprník*, then *perník* as we know it today. Gingerbread shaped or "printed" by molds was later replaced by simpler shaped gingerbread figures decorated with icing. We might also try gingerbread figures that have been freely shaped by hand, "*drůbeřka*" (which used to be just a mixture of flour and water used as modelling material for children's toys – nowadays this name is mainly used for gingerbread shaped for the most part by hand and woven into strands). Iced gingerbread figures are nowadays very popular – it is just a matter of taste and skill for them to remain the works of folk art that humbly decorate our festivities to this day.

Gingerbread for shaping

500 g plain rye flour (may be replaced by 00 grade plain wheat flour)
250 g icing sugar
2 tbsps cocoa
half a coffee spoon baking soda (bicarbonate of soda)

finely ground spices – star anise, cinnamon, cloves, allspice, fennel, aniseed, vanilla, cardamom, lemon peel, coriander and a pinch of pepper

Mix all the loose ingredients well. It is a good idea to heat them up to room temperature. Prepare a cup of honey that has been heated in water, two whole eggs and two tablespoons of rum, and whisk them all thoroughly. With this mixture knead the flour into firm smooth dough. At first this will not appear possible, but you will eventually manage to combine all the ingredients and to work them all on the pastry board into a velvety dough. If you add any more liquid, you might well be able to knead the dough better, but then it will spread out as it is baked. Wrap a little loaf of this dough in a freezer bag and place out in the cold for several days.

Then knead the dough again on the pastry board, rolling it out flat until it is as thick as straw, cut out the shapes and store loose (so that they do not get baked together) on a tray that has been thinly greased with oil or pure bees' wax. Slowly bake until golden. Do not burn! Before baking, the gingerbread figures should be glazed with egg yolks mixed in a little rum, or after baking, while still hot, with dextrin syrup - i.e. synthetic resin from fruit trees dissolved in water, which is edible and harmless. Postage stamps used to be gummed with dextrin. It used to be available at large drugstores in the form of a yellow powder, but nowadays it is not so easy to find. The advantage of dextrin was that the albumen glaze did not flake off the gingerbread.

Icing to decorate gingerbread figures

1 egg white
approx 200-250 g icing sugar sifted through a fine sieve
one coffee spoon lemon juice
2 heaped tbsps of Solamyl starch powder

Mix well, fill a plastic bag, cut off a corner with sharp scissors to form a tiny opening and you are ready to start decorating. The consistency of the icing can only be determined through practice - precise instructions on the quantity of sugar and flour cannot be given. When the little cone is gently squeezed the icing should form a smooth thin line that sits nicely on the surface - it should neither be runny nor "hang" in the air.

Apple strudel (Jablkový závin or more accurately štrúdl)

Christmas Eve without fragrant apple strudel is quite unimaginable in many families. After all, apples and dishes made from apples have always been part and parcel

of Christmas festivities.

There is nothing simple about the preparation of classic apple strudel. My mum always thought back both with horror and a little affection to her mother-in-law's strudel, whose dough was prepared in her household with the addition of raw rabbit suet. Of course, this had to be rolled out beforehand with a rolling pin until it frothed. After this arduous alchemy the strudel was said to be unbelievably soft and flaky.

320 g plain flour
2 dcl lukewarm water
1 tsp vinegar, a pinch of salt, 1 tbsp of dripping (or that suet!)
1 egg

Knead into a smooth dough. Shape into a little loaf, place this in a small heated pan and leave for half an hour. Cover in a clean teacloth, sprinkle with flour, roll out the dough flat and then stretch it out by hand into a very thin sheet. Sprinkle this with white breadcrumbs fried in butter, on which you place a layer of peeled, sliced apples, add raisins and walnut kernels, sprinkle with cinnamon and add heated butter. Lift the teacloth at one end with both hands and roll up the strudel, closing off the ends properly. Using the teacloth, place the strudel on a greased tray, brush it with cream and bake in a hot oven until golden. Then sprinkle well with vanilla sugar and slice it up. The main thing is not to get angry when the strudel disappears before you've managed to make the Christmas punch.

Crumbly apple pie (Křehký jablkový koláč)

You could try an alternative type of apple cake. This has the advantage of being prepared a day before, which will certainly be appreciated by busy housewives who don't know where to start on Christmas Eve. It is similar to the famous English apple pie, but Czechified a little.

Crumble up the fat into the flour and add baking powder, vanilla sugar, eggs, lemon peel and juice and a drop of cold water as required. Knead into a smooth dough and leave to rest for a while in the cold. Peel the apples and grate them with a coarse grater, sprinkle with a little sugar, cinammon and raisins soaked in rum, and you can also add sliced walnuts and mix them all together with vanilla custard powder. Divide the dough up into two parts and roll both of them out flat. One of them will form the bottom of the pie in a round tray or a ceramic baking dish with high sides. Heap in the apple mix, level it off, cover with the other piece of flattened dough, pinch the edges together, snip off any extra dough and then decoratively crimp the edges with your fingers. With the remaining dough you can create various embellishments on top (e.g. stripes, leaves, roses or flowers). Pierce the surface, so that the steam can rise from the apples while baking. Bake until golden, then leave to cool (so that the custard in amongst the apples can set) and sprinkle with sugar.

Lemon puff pastry

Two cups of flour – one semi-coarse
and the other plain flour
1 sachet vanilla sugar
1/8 kg butter
1 sachet baking powder
1 pinch of salt
1 egg
finely grated peel from half a well-washed lemon
juice from half a lemon and a little cold water if required

Filling

Half a kilo of coarsely grated peeled apples, sugar to taste (the less the better), cinammon, raisins presoaked in rum and nuts, 1 sachet of vanilla custard powder, mix well and fill the pie.

Bear's paws (Medvědí tlapky)

Various Christmas cakes, pies, "feather beds" (*peřinky*) and sourdough breads traditionally used to be baked at humble hearths during Christmases gone by. If cookies (*cukroví*, formerly *pokroutky*) were prepared for

children and carol singers they were very modest. They never dreamt of the many varied kinds that we have today, bursting with fat and sugar. In urban families, where little Christmas trees first started to be "dressed" in the first half of the 19th century, they needed to bake cookies not only for the punch table, but also to hang on the tree. It is not the aim of this modest little book to provide Christmas cookie recipes – you surely have many of your own already, perhaps passed down within your family – and it is through this very handing-down from generation to generation that they have been refined to absolute perfection. But just to make sure that within the narrative context of Christmas past we do not lack for cookie recipes, there will at least be some instructions here on popular Christmas cookies, fragrant and above all properly matured. Unfortunately, most confectionery does not last this long, for once it is discovered in its secret hiding place, it is almost entirely nibbled away on the sly...

350 g flour, 250 g butter, 180 g sugar, 100 g ground almonds, 2 tbsps of cocoa or grated chocolate, 2 egg yolks, 5 ground cloves, cinammon and lemon peel.

Press the dough thinly into metal "little paw" moulds and bake until golden. Pour in the hot vanilla sugar, ideally store in a metal box or other receptacle and leave for at least fourteen days.

Vanilla crescents (Vanilkové rohlíčky)

Perhaps the most popular lovely white confectionery of all, filling your home with its vanilla fragrance. Every time that I sprinkle vanilla sugar on my baking it conjures up the Christmas of my childhood and I am reminded of these crumbly crescents that my mum used to shape with her work-worn hands into unbelievably elaborate forms.

150 g plain flour, 20 g icing sugar, 110 g butter, 50 g ground peeled roasted almonds, 1 egg yolk, half a crushed vanilla bean, lemon peel, vanilla icing sugar for the covering.

Knead well and cut off pieces from a thin roll of dough to form little horns. Some do this by pressing the dough into little metal pastry cutters, but truth to tell, there is no real substitute for the hand-made ones. Place on a thinly greased tray and bake until golden. While still hot, cover in vanilla icing sugar.

Ginger cookies (Zázvorky)

The traditional folk Christmas tree was redolent of ginger cookies, and because they are not only shaped, but also decorated by pricks, wavy lines, circles and the like, they are also very decorative.

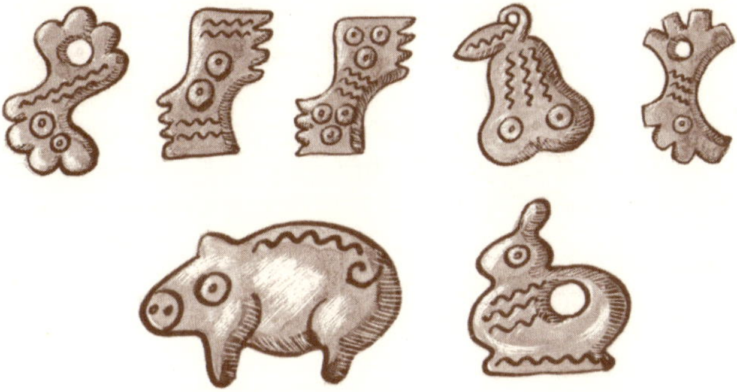

4 whole eggs, 500 g sugar, 500 g flour (half semi-coarse and half plain) and two heaped teaspoons of grated ginger.

Whisk the eggs and the sugar in a bowl (for about a quarter of an hour) then add the flour and ginger. Knead the dough and roll out flat about half a centimetre in width. Cut out shapes with various cutters and decorate as the fancy takes you. Place on a thinly greased tray and leave to dry out for at least half a day. Then bake intensively for about a quarter of an hour (at a high temperature the ginger cookies "leap up") and slowly dry out at a low temperature for half an hour. You could try out this recipe for the first time with a half portion.

Cockchafers (Chróste)

Wherever they harvest a bumper autumn crop of walnuts they can treat themselves to this ancient confectionery from the Haná region.

140 g sugar, 140 g ground nuts, 30 g white breadcrumbs, snow from two or three egg whites, a little rum, lemon peel.

Mix these ingredients together lightly into a firm egg white snow, then form dollops with a tablespoon on a waxed tray and bake in a gently heated oven.

24

Linz cookies (Slepované hvězdičky)

There should be no lack of what are known as Linz cookies among traditional confectionery. They are pleasantly sourish and so make a welcome change to the other cookies, which are mostly very sweet.

400 g plain flour, 280 g butter, 140 g sugar, 2 egg yolks, lemon peel, vanilla.

Crumble the butter into the flour, add all the other ingredients and knead into a smooth dough. Leave this "loaf" to lie for a while in the cold. Then roll it out flat until it is as thick as straw and cut out stars or flowers. Leave half of these shapes intact and cut out "windows" with a thimble from the other half. Line them up on a tray (which need not be greased) and bake in a medium hot oven. After they have been baked, carefully place them on a smooth-surfaced mat and once they have cooled, the full shapes are brushed with blackcurrant preserve and stuck to their "windowed" tops. These should be allowed to mature for at least a week.

Crackling cookies (Škvarkové cukroví)

Popular country cookies. Three weeks before Christmas old aunts in Vysočina used to say it was time to make "some o' them *šišmáčky* for the young 'uns". These tasty cookies had to be left out to mature.

300 g plain flour, 250 g ground crackling, 150 g sugar, two tablespoons cocoa, 1 whole egg, a tsp of cinammon, a ground clove and grated lemon peel.

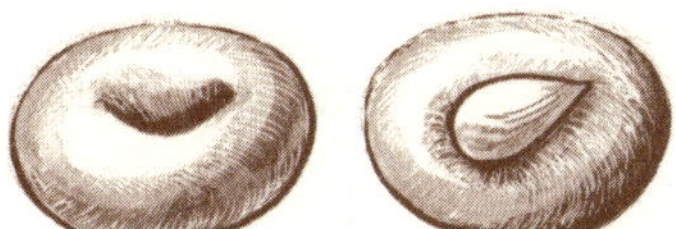

Form little balls out of smooth, well-kneaded dough, make little hollows in them, press almonds, hazelnuts or walnuts into these hollows and bake until golden. Coat in vanilla sugar while still warm.

Snow cookies (Sněhové pečivo)

These snow cookies used to be made as Christmas tree decorations, either in the form of pink and white wreaths (rings) dyed with "Breton" (a foodstuff dye used at that time) or as snow meringues decorated with a nozzled cone in a zigzag pattern and placed on a greased tray. This way a snow chain was formed, which looked very attractive on the tree. Snow cookies are decorated with a linen or similar cone with a decorative nozzle on an oiled tray and baked very slowly, or rather dried, in an oven. The advantage of these decorative cookies is that you can use up the egg whites left over from your other baking preparations. Count on some 60 g of granulated sugar and one soup-spoon of icing sugar per egg white. Whisk up the egg whites together with the granulated sugar in a pot. Place this pot on a receptacle containing boiling

water, so that it sits above the steam, and carry on whisking until the snow has completely thickened (success depends on the firmness of the snow). Then take the pot away and whisk the weighed-out icing sugar, fill the cone and immediately make circles, S-shapes, eights, meringues or a chain and leave to dry out in the oven.

Fruit sauce (Muzika, odvárka, Tomáškový kompot, vocet)

Again a reminder of times gone by. This delicious thin fruit purée used to be prepared by housewives as early as 21st December, the feast of St. Thomas, hence the name. But nobody was allowed to taste it until Christmas Eve. Why *muzika*? Well, because all the treats from the larder come to the dance here – dried fruit, raisins, almonds, nuts and rum. Why *vocet* (vinegar)? Perhaps because of its sharp taste, which was welcomed at Chrismas feasts as an appetizer. *Odvárka* used to be brewed up everywhere and we can assume that it was popular from the variety of the names alone.

Wash dried pears, desiccated apples (even sour ones) and dried plums and boil together with star anise, whole cinammon, a strip of lemon peel, a piece of vanilla and cloves.

Press the soft-boiled fruit and add sugar to taste. You can thicken with grated gingerbread, add the raisins, peeled roasted almonds and walnut kernels and don't forget the rum. Leave the mixture out for several days. *Muzika* used to be consumed both hot and cold and even with meat in times gone by, later more with Christmas cake or all on its own...

Mushroom and barley casserole ("Černý Kuba - mastná huba")

A traditional Christmas Eve meal in the Giant Mountains, though it also used to be eaten elsewhere and at other times. Mix soft-boiled dried mushrooms plus salt and caraway with the water in which they were boiled (but not too much) and boiled pearl barley or peeled barley. This barley may also be successfully substituted by ground buckwheat. First boil the barley in salted water with a tablespoon of dripping or oil. This does not apply to buckwheat because all you need to do with that is scald it in the boiling salty mushroom water and leave it to stand covered for 25 minutes. The water will be absorbed into the buckwheat. The mixture of barley or buckwheat and sliced mushrooms is seasoned with pressed garlic, pepper, marjoram, dripping and crackling

and placed in a greased baking tray. Bake until golden. Dark mushrooms (rough-stemmed boletus) were used, hence "black" Kuba. However, in some places they became hardened and added boiled blood or dark smoked meat, though of course this was no longer fasting fare.

Mushroom soufflé (Hubník)

Similar to Černý Kuba, originally from Vysočina. Pour the salted water from the boiled mushrooms onto a diced bread roll, add sliced soft mushrooms, dripping, garlic, marjoram and egg yolks - mix it all well in. Finally, gently mix in hardened snow from egg whites. Fill a greased breadcrumb-strewn baking tray and bake until golden. The bread roll sometimes used to be substituted by salted semolina pudding to form the basis of this mushroom soufflé. This bread roll variety of mushroom fasting food seems to me to be lighter on stomachs that have to contend with Christmas feasting.

Millet gruel (Jahelník)

Jahelník is traditional old Christmas Eve fare, to which people used to ascribe magic powers, believing that the little yellow millet grains would bring an abundance of money in the forthcoming year to all those who ate it.

Examine the fine yellow millet grains and pick out any impurities, scald, rinse in cold water and boil in a mixture of approximately two cups of millet, a half litre of water, a half litre of milk, half a tablespoon of salt, four sugar cubes, a little cinammon, crushed or grated nutmeg and two tablespoons of oil. Boil slowly until soft. Mix in sugar, a knob of butter, cream (if the boiled millet is too dry), egg yolks, raisins, dried plums and well-washed dried apricots. Into the moulds (dishes) brushed with butter pour the mixture and cook as a soufflé. If you have enough egg whites left over, whisk up some sweet snow and layer it onto the baking *jahelník*. Leave to brown for a while until you see the golden mountain peaks!

Feather beds, oven loafers (Peřinky, peciválky)

This ancient fare was also traditionally on our ancestors' Christmas Eve table. Three days beforehand bake little buns (similar to the well-known ducat buns) from well-yeasted dough. Before serving, scald them in boiling milk, butter them and sweeten with honey or sugar. They may also be sprinkled with "*prachanda*" (known elsewhere as "*pracharanda*", i.e. dried pears ground up in a mortar) or grated gingerbread. Elsewhere they were sprinkled with poppy seed, and an interesting thick, sweet poppy-seed sauce was even concocted. What

a treat! And all those calories!

When there was not enough time to shape these little *peciválky* individually, they simply baked one large bun, which was then cut up into quarters...

Home-made bread (Domácí chleba)

Bread was never allowed to be lacking from our ancestors' Christmas Eve table. It was a symbol of plenty, a basic foodstuff, and people valued it greatly. Perhaps many of you will remember a grandmother who always made the sign of the cross over the loaf before cutting it. The baking of bread was always accompanied by numerous preparations, superstitions and magic.

Nowadays we can only dream of fragrant home-baked bread with a white floury crust, with a little ember from the oven occasionally baked in, bread that had to last for three weeks. But it is no dream to try to bake your own bread. Nothing used to be weighed out, as an experienced housewife measured everything out in handfuls "by eye". Each

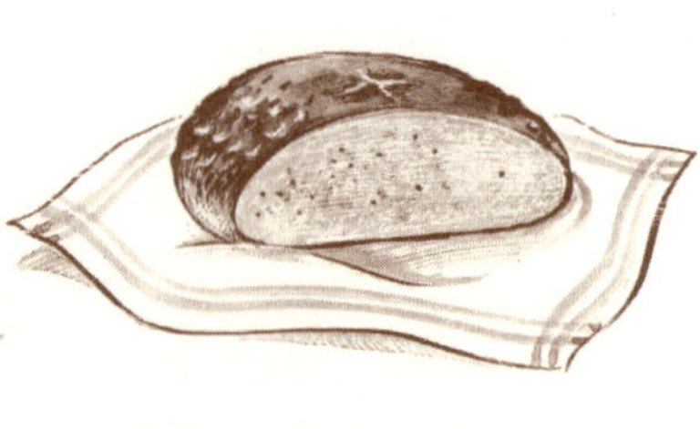

loaf comprised a two-litre jug of hot water, half a handful of caraway, a handful of salt and one bread basket of flour, normally a mixture of rye and wheat flour. Sourdough preserved from the last baking session (known as "*nátěstek*", i.e. mother dough) was used. This was rejuvenated with hot water, some of the weighed-out flour was added and the mixture was left for an appropriate time to rise. Then the remaining water and flour was added to the other ingredients. One went round the kneading trough with a stirrer and the dough was mixed. After the dough had risen, it was divided up and shaped into loaves, which were again left to rise in heated, flour-strewn bread baskets. Before being baked, each loaf had its surface washed with lukewarm water. It was then blessed and placed in the oven with a shovel.

Nowadays we have to make do with a cooker oven and few of us have the opportunity to buy real leaven, which can only be found these days in the foothills of the Giant Mountains, where they use it to make their popular *Kyselo* soup. Sometimes a taste that is similar to that of leaven is attained if you leave out the sourdough from the yeast to ferment with some extra bread crust for several hours, or even better overnight.

1 kg plain flour (wheat and rye), 600 ml lukewarm water, 60 g yeast, 3 teaspoons of caraway, 3 tsps of salt, 3 tbsps of vinegar.

Make leaven out of yeast, two sugar cubes, a little lukewarm water and a handful of flour. Knead together with the other ingredients into a hard dough. Cover and leave to rise in the warmth. Then work it over on the pastry board, make a cone or loaf shape and again leave to rise in a bread basket. Then tip it out onto a flour-strewn tray, wash the surface in lukewarm water and place in a heated oven. Bake for approx. 45–50 minutes. As soon as it is baked, again wipe the surface of the loaf with lukewarm salty water.

32 Cabbage soup (Kapustnica)

This very distinctive tasting soup traditionally used to be on the tables of our Slovak neighbours on Christmas Eve. In eastern Slovakia they also used to make it, suitably strong of course, for weddings and other long-lasting celebrations at which some alcohol-induced fatigue might be anticipated. Kapustnica is said to put the dead back on their feet. This is perhaps due to the sauerkraut brine, which is added to the soup together with the cabbage, or it is just faith – who knows? But one thing is for sure: this soup will appeal without distinction both to teetotallers and to those who don't deny themselves a drop or two.

The preparations for cabbage soup only appear complicated. Cook smoked meat (brisket), bones (pickings), bacon rind, smoked pork knuckle and the like. Together with the meat cook a whole onion, several sprigs of thyme, several bay leaves, a couple of allspice and juniper berries and black peppercorns. Take out the soft meat and leave to cool. Heat the

bacon in a largish saucepan and stir-fry sufficient onion until red, add a slice of paprika sausage and dried mushrooms presoaked in water and milk, sprinkle all this with sweet and hot red pepper and add the strained broth from the meat. Simmer for a while and add good chopped (ideally home-made) sauerkraut with its brine. Cook until the sauerkraut is soft. Add salt and season as required with soup spices. The soup is then thickened with flour mixed in with a little of the cold broth. Of course, proper Slovak Christmas Eve cabbage soup only has cabbage, mushrooms and paprika. Smoked meat and sausage would not be suitable for the fasting period. But if we do not take this too strictly then we can add a little sausage to the soup or even heat up that cooked meat that has previously been diced. Just like sirloin or goulash, the soup is better if it has been "left to lie" for at least a day.

Some like to add a tablespoon of sour cream. And brown bread goes well with cabbage soup.

Fried peas (Pučálka)

This is made out of sprouted peas, which during the Middle Ages were not only Lenten fare, but also a welcome treat during winter flax spinning parties, feather stripping sessions and other social gatherings. Because peas were an essential part of the Christmas Eve menu with the magic number of nine dishes, it was on the table either in the form of soup, pottage or the popular *pučálka*.

Soak the picked unpeeled peas overnight in cold water. Strain the swollen peas and spread out in a shallow dish, cover and leave to pregerminate in the heat. When the sprouts are at least 6 mm in length, dry-roast the peas (as fasting fare) or sauté them in oil, dripping or butter, adding salt and pepper. With their attraction to taste combinations that we find unusual, people in the Middle Ages sweetened *pučálka* with honey and added pepper. From raw pea or lentil *pučálka* you can prepare a tasty and very healthy salad by adding a finely chopped shallot onion, oil and vinegar dressing (vinegar, sugar, salt and water).

Christmas Eve carp (Štědrovečerní kapr)

Fish is good and healthy in every respect, though here in the Czech lands we don't eat it as often as we should. Christmas Eve carp is a great delicacy. If only there weren't any of that killing...But that can't be helped – fish out the fish from the bathtub – it's best to wrap it in a teacloth while it is still in the water, so that it does not slip out of your hand. Place on a board and soundly hit it on the head with a mallet and then immediately cut with a knife behind its head, so that the blood drains off and the meat remains white. Carefully slit the stomach, taking out the innards – but be careful of the gall bladder. Cut that out immediately

together with the surrounding innards, which might be bitter. Then remove the intestines - you can make use of the remaining good innards in soup. The scales from the fish are removed very simply by running your fingers against the direction of their growth. Then rub the fish thoroughly in coarse salt, wash well in cold water and dry with a paper towel. Cut portions thinly, salt, sprinkle with lemon, place in a dish and leave to stand for 12–24 hours in the fridge. It is a good idea to "rearrange" the fish portions at least once, so that the ones at the bottom are not too salty.

Just before you fry it, coat the fish in breadcrumbs (dipped in whisked eggs and flour) and slowly and thoroughly fry in a substantial layer of fat - i.e. oil, or even better, dripping. My grandmother used to say that if a couple of slices of raw carrot are added to the hot fat then it will not burn. Place the all-round golden-fried fish onto paper napkins to absorb any excess fat. Only then can you nicely arrange it on a heated dish, adding a couple of lemon segments and a sprig of curly parsley. Meanwhile the head of the family will doubtless be preparing a chilled festive white wine...

Fish soup (Rybí polévka)

Clean the carp innards well, drench in milk and put out in the cold. Remove the gills (opercula) from the carp's head. It may just be slander, but they are said to make the soup bitter. That is what my grandmother taught me and I never had the courage to try cooking the head with the gills, so I don't know... Rub the heads in salt, wash well in clean cold water and place in slightly acidified and salted boiling water with onion, bay leaf, allspice and pepper. Cook for some time on a low boil, but do not overcook – the fish is ready very quickly. Strain the broth and pick the meat from the heads after they have cooled. Froth up the onion in oil or butter and brown the sliced or diced root vegetables (carrots, parsley, celery or leek). Pour off the broth from the heads and briefly simmer, adding nutmeg or mace, a little ginger and a little soup spice, and after simmering for a while add a yellow butter roux mixed well in cold water. Boil the innards (liver and milt) separately in salty water. This is worthwhile because you will then manage to save the soup if the innards leave an aftertaste of bile, which can sometimes happen even when the greatest care is taken. Cut up the cooked innards into small pieces and together with the broth add to the soup. If you manage to acquire some nice mature roe, add salt and cook in butter, as it has a fine orange colour. Cook and mix with a little milk or cold water and add to the soup together with the meat from the heads. Finally, you can make the fish soup taste mellower with cream and a whipped egg yolk and season with chopped green parsley and a teaspoon of butter. Butter and dice a bread roll to go with the fish soup.

Buttered fish (Ryba na másle)

Carp on the Christmas table is a fairly recent tradition. In the past fish for fasting was only indulged in at monasteries, by wealthy burghers and the nobility. Country folk rarely had fish. Normally they baked bread in the shape of a fish. Nowadays Christmas carp is taken for granted, even though it is not all that inexpensive an affair - but Christmas without fish? Of course, some people cannot indulge in this fried treat because of their diet. In that case you could prepare buttered carp for them. Salt a cleaned half carp, sprinkle with lemon, brush with butter and caraway. Then cook in the oven until red, occasionally pouring on the well-prepared juice. You might even sprinkle on some flour and add a little water, so that the butter does not burn. To go with fish cooked in butter, boil potatoes, add hot butter and sprinkle with green parsley. You can prepare tench, trout and pike in the same way, as well as fillet and the great majority of all freshwater and sea fish. Fish that has only been salted and sprinkled with lemon juice and cooked in butter loses none of its characteristic taste. It is quickly prepared and tastes marvellous.

Black carp (Kapr na černo)

This unusual recipe again involves medieval cuisine, in which meat prepared with sweet, strongly seasoned sauces predominates. Use was made of honey, gingerbread, dried fruit, spices, beer and wine. Such recipes are now a rather old-fashioned rarity, and apart from Polish wine sauce and Wallachian blackthorn sauce ("*trnčená máčka*") on smoked meat, only this black sauce for fish remains popular. Although it is quite demanding, many families still prepare it for Christmas.

You need blood from the carp; if you do not manage to catch any when you kill it, rinse out the gutted fish with vinegar, and keep this in a mug. Boil a litre of water in a pot, add salt, one largish carrot, a stick of celery, two largish onions, 10 peppercorns, 10 allspice berries, a piece of ginger (whole or crushed), 4 cloves, 2 bay leaves, a sprig of thyme (dried acceptable), 2 sage leaves, 8 dried plums, lemon peel and 2 slices of lemon without the white pith and pips, and a handful of raisins. Cook slowly, making sure that all the ingredients are thoroughly done.

Strain and cook the carp in a broth on a gentle bubbling simmer. Do not overcook – the fish is ready very quickly! Carefully place in a baking dish. Press all the fruit, vegetables and spice that was boiled in the broth, which is then to be strained again to make sure there are no bones from the fish, and add a quarter litre of sweet dark beer, a little dark caramel sugar, a tablespoon of elderberry or blueberry preserve to improve the colour, thicken with grated gingerbread or grated hard brown bread, add the vinegar used to rinse out the fish and cook for some time. Finally, add 1–2 dl of red wine and a tablespoon of butter, but then stop cooking. The sauce is tastier if it is left to stand for at least one day. Garnish the fish in the baking dish with slivers of butter and cook, while preferably heating the pan of sauce in a pan of water. Good homemade bread dumplings go well with this old Czech carp.

Jellied fish or blue carp (Ryba v rosolu, kapr na modro)

My grandmother and mother always used to come out winning from Christmas thanks to their carp in transparent jelly, embellished with boiled carrots and egg white florettes and leek leaves. Goodness only knows where they found the time for all that! In those days they used to make brawn out of calf trotters. The preparation was challenging and complex, so for many years I refused to perform such pointless conjuring tricks, until recently when curiosity got the better of me and I tried to prepare carp "under glass", in a slightly simpler way to be sure, but with a result that is pleasantly surprising.

How to go about it? Cook the fish for a short time in acidified water with onion and seasoning (bay leaf, allspice and black pepper). The fish should turn a nice blue. Do not overcook! Carefully take it out and place neatly in a glass dish or fish pan. Prepare these embellishments from cooked vegetables and eggs – stars, florettes, leaves and hearts. Wash out the broth from the fish with snow from the egg whites, which you can then mix back into the hot fish broth and leave to set. Strain through clean coarse cheesecloth and add a measured quantity of pre-rinsed swollen gelatine (20–30 g per litre of liquid). Heat the broth, but do not boil. Leave to cool a little, add vinegar

and salt and slowly pour over the fish. Decorate with vegetables and pour on the rest of the liquid. Leave out to cool. The jelly should be translucent, firm but soft, and taste pleasantly tart. If you want to tip out the finished jelly into the dish, you have to arrange the decorations at the bottom of the receptacle into which a little liquid jelly has been poured, and then arrange the fish bottom

down and pour in the remainder of the liquid after some time. Before tipping out the fish, heat up the receptacle briefly, so that this little beauty slips off its sides nicely.

Carp with sage (Kapr na šalvěji)

This unusual preparation for carp has been passed down from generation to generation in our family. It is a really very old recipe, even though its origins are certainly not to be found in the country cottage. Cut up a cleaned and gutted fish lengthways across the stomach, then prepare it in a baking dish as you would skate, i.e. with the back sticking up. Interlard the entire fish with leaves of fresh sage and spread thickly with anchovy butter. In the past they had to arduously rub salted anchovies with butter. Nowadays we are spared this work thanks to anchovy paste. Fry onion in oil or butter until red, along with carrot, celery and parsley and spread out the fish on this base. Cook in a well-heated oven, occasionally pouring on the well-prepared juice and adding a little water beneath as required. Boiled potatoes go well with fish prepared in this way. The aroma and taste of fish with sage is inimitable and outstanding.

Potato salad (Bramborový salát)

Classic potato salad has numerous alternative tastes, depending on family tradition and how you'd rather have it. Select the potatoes for your salad carefully - same type, same size, undamaged and ideally an oily variety that does not boil to mush. These used to be called "crescents" (*rohlíčky*). Cook in their skins in salted water. After straining, rinse in cold water and leave to cool, then peel. Prepare hard-boiled eggs, carrot, celery and parsley cooked in salted water, sour gherkin, peeled onion, canned green peas and peeled apples. Dice the potatoes. Dice the other ingredients into even smaller pieces. You might even add finely sliced ham salami to the salad. Mix all of this gently but well - "dry" in advance. Then mix in the mayonnaise prepared from high quality bought mayonnaise ("*majolka*"), two tablespoons of full-fat mustard and two tablespoons of oil. Add salt, lemon juice, white pepper, 3–4 tablespoons of white yoghurt (if the salad is not to be too rich and heavy). Mix well. Then gently mix in the loose ingredients. Taste (and get others to taste) and add salt, lemon juice or a drop of vinegar as required by the comments of the other tasters and your own taste. Do not mix for too long, or the salad will become a mayonnaise mush. The salad is best if it is left to stand for at least half a day in the cold, but not in the fridge.

You can prepare a light potato salad as a side dish from hot or cold boiled potatoes, onions, oil, vinegar and salt. Slice the onions finely, mix in with slices of potato and a dressing made up of a pinch of sugar, salt, a teaspoon of vinegar and 2–3 tablespoons of oil. You may add cut chives and boiled eggs.

Festive Christmas Day roast sirloin (Slavnostní svíčková pečeně k Hodu Božímu)

Roast sirloin is an age-old gem among the jewels of traditional Czech cuisine. Best of all, of course, is sirloin from a leg of venison. The meat should be cured in advance.

Clean the demembraned meat, dry with a napkin and lard with small wedges of good bacon. Place in an earthenware pot, garnish with slices of onion and carrots, add sliced celery and parsley, bay leaves, allspice, black peppercorns, a sprig of thyme and a thin strip of lemon peel. Prepare the marinade – add three tablespoons of oil to some red wine and two tablespoons of vinegar and pour this mixture onto the meat. Place a washed fir sprig on top and secure everything as firmly as possible beneath a weighted lid – you could even put a rock on top, if you clean it properly and place it in a plastic bag. If the meat is not entirely steeped in the marinade you should turn it over at least once, so that it marinates on all sides and leave it to stand for at least two days. Then take out the meat from the brine and quickly roast it on all sides in butter. Only then should you salt it well, add a little of the juice from the brine below and stew under a lid in the oven. Cook the remaining vegetables, seasoning and marinade until the vegetables are soft and the seasoning is cooked thoroughly. At the same time use the marinade to baste the roast. Then strain the vegetables and seasoning. Take out the soft meat, sprinkle the dripping with flour and leave to roast for a while, then add the strained vegetables and marinade and cook it all thoroughly. Meanwhile burn several sugar cubes to make a darkish caramel, boil in a little water and add to the sauce. Finally add a good sweet or sour cream to the sauce plus salt, lemon juice or sugar to taste. Do not cook any longer and add a teaspoon of fresh butter to taste. The sauce should be creamy with a pleasantly sourish taste. If you prepare the roast sirloin in advance, before serving heat up the sauce in water, cut the cold meat with a sharp knife, place in a fire-resistant dish, add a tablespoon of water plus slivers of butter on top and start roasting. Separately set out the meat in its dish, the sauce in the sauce boat and the well-done dumplings. Serve onto plates at the table – there is nothing more

off-putting than soggy dumplings swamped in sauce or meat chastely hiding under the sauce. Only at a station restaurant can that liberty be taken. Festive roast sirloin goes together with pear halves (either preserved or very soft butter pears) peeled with a nice hollow at the core, into which you can pile in the cranberry preserve with a tablespoon and a half-slice of lemon. I need not stress that a high quality red wine goes well with this regal dish as a matter of course, and because this roast is called *svíčková* ("candle roast"), candle illumination and flowers on the table are also appropriate.

St. Stephen's goose (Svatoštěpanská husa)

Another great delicacy of old Czech cuisine cannot be spoilt, except perhaps by burning or oversalting, but that will surely never happen to you. Modern-day fast-food poultry is cooked more speedily than in the past, when enormous force-fed geese had to be steamed for a long time beforehand in a *dušák* ("steamer" – a double baking pan). Clean the goose of any remaining feathers, wash, dry with a napkin, sprinkling in salt and caraway. Place inside a heated oven, so that the meat gets a "thermal shock", contracts and so does not release any liquid, keeping the bird juicy. After the goose has been cooked for several minutes, sprinkle salt and caraway on the surface and add a little hot water underneath. At first cook under cover and then after some 45 to 60 minutes, take the lid off, take some well-done dripping from roasted fatty pork, add two or three small sour apples to the goose and brush the surface with a mixture of dark beer and a teaspoonful of honey. Then keep cooking the goose without a lid, so that it has nicely red and crispy crackling. Old Czech goose goes well with soft potato dumplings, good home-made sauerkraut or red cabbage from a head of cabbage and of course, beer too after all! Gall bladder beware.

NEW YEAR DRINKS (NOVOROČNÍ NÁPOJE)

We traditionally let in the New Year with good resolutions, and wishes of health, happiness and contentment to all those around us – always with a toast, of course.

Beer, wine and the old spirits go together well with ceremonial occasions, and it is not the fault of these drinks that some people are unable to enjoy them within reason.

Mulled caramel wine (Hriaté)

A drink that is eminently suitable for a winter idyll when we come home early on a frosty evening and need something to warm us up.

Burn a few sugar cubes to a golden brown caramel, pour on a little water and add three cloves, a piece of whole cinammon and a thin slice of well-washed lemon peel (some also add a piece of vanilla pod). Boil for a while and then prepare a good slivovitz (pear brandy or calvados) in a glass and pour in the aromatic infusion. Place a metal teaspoon in the glass just to be sure. In the Wallachian-Slovak border area where they brew this fine beverage they also add some melted bacon, which nicely "beds out" the stomach for a quota of alcohol. There you have it – there's no accounting for taste.

Mulled wine (Svařené víno)

This pleasant winter drink imbued with good cheer can be a real treat, but it can also be ruined good and proper if you don't know how to go about it. Let some sugar burn until it is golden, pour on a little water and add seasoning - whole cinammon, cloves, star anise, a cardamom pod, a piece of lemon peel and orange peel with the white pith removed. Heat until small white bubbles appear on the surface. Then remove immediately and pour into heat-resistant glasses. You could put a half-slice of lemon or orange into the glass. Never burn the wine – the term "*svařené*" víno is a little misleading. If you really do scald the wine, you will certainly get a hot liquid, but quite free of alcohol, which will have evaporated. If you embellish the drink with a trace of good cherry brandy or apricot brandy, you will reap much-deserved praise, but then *svařák*, as it is known, will knock you off your feet and should be drunk carefully...

Fragrant Christmas tea (Vánoční voňavý čaj)

Do not throw out the peel from apples that you have previously washed. Dry it and you can then make an excellent infusion - pour on boiling water, add a piece of whole cinammon and two cloves and leave to infuse. Then sweeten with honey, flavour with a little lemon juice and a tea to fragrance your entire home is all ready. And no harm will surely be done if you add a drop of rum.

CHRISTMAS FOLK-CUSTOM ARTIFACTS (VÁNOČNÍ ZVYKOSLOVNÉ PŘEDMĚTY)

For over a thousand years Czech culture has taken shape under the influence of Christianity. Early Christianity 51
timed its important festivals to coincide with pagan cult ceremonies in an effort to stem the influence of pagan tradition on people's awareness. But these efforts by the church were only successful to some degree. It was more successful in covering up the old customs and merging them in with the new official Christian festivals. This is also the case with Christmas. The fusion of both phenomena – the popular traditions of pre-Christian times and the new perception of the world under the influence of the church – shaped the unique form taken by the Czech

Christmas. This fusion of meanings is also evident in the objects that are associated with Christmas, which are nowadays referred to in Czech as "*zvykoslovné*". These traditional folk artifacts were created just before the occasion they were to mark and were then dispatched during the ceremony concerned, either by consumption or by ceremonial burning and the like. For these reasons

very little material evidence remains, though drawings by Professor Karel Rozum, who at the end of the 19th century portrayed the final remains of these objects, whether tiny structures made of fruit, bread and twigs or Advent figures doing their rounds, are of great value.

Just as customs, ceremonies and annual traditions were not only there as entertainments, but derived their meaning primarily from their effects on the weather and the future prosperity, good housekeeping, health, life and fortunes of the individual, so the traditional folk artifacts involved in these ceremonies were not just soulless decorations, but they had their hard and fast meaning, symbolism and function.

It is not such a complex matter to revive these objects and restore their message from remote times down to the present day, but it is all the better to know their original meaning and to respect their basic colour, materials and symbols. This way they can enhance our festivities to this day, bring us happiness from our own creativity and make the Christmas atmosphere at home pleasant and aromatic.

Traditional means of expression in folk symbolism

The symbols of life, light, health and happiness: the green tree and branch, the red apple, the full egg, colourful fabrics, baked figures, and candles.

Symbols of fertility, wealth, abundance and acquisition of property: peas, lentils, dried fruit and mushrooms, grain, rosehip, poppyheads, nuts, and sourdough bread.

Symbols protecting buildings, people, livestock and fields: bread, garlic, salt, honey, thorns, thorn switches, magic herbs, sanctified branches and food, and the colour red.

Symbols of death, ruination and indignity: threshed straw (without ears), empty shells (empty white eggs, snail shells), broken candles, and the colour white (though of course this is also the colour of purity).

Nicholas plait (Mikulášský vrkoč)

Weave yeast dough (similar to that of Christmas cake but a little more "short-measured"), into a three-strand braid and wind up into a garland on a greased baking tray. Brush with a whisked egg yolk, bake and leave to stand for one or two days. Prepare six 15–20 cm long sticks that have been sharpened at both ends and run them through pieces of dried fruit: plums, pears, apples, figs and apricots. Insert the sticks into the garland and tie round with bast fibre at the top. Then stick a large red apple on top, from the upper part of which six smaller skewers with impaled raisins are to radiate out. On the outer tips of the skewers stick rosehips or small poppyheads, for example, and festoon them with a little chain of swollen peas threaded on with the aid of a threading needle. You can crown the whole work with little bits and pieces (a poppy head, a bird made of dough, dried fruit and a twig of *Krušpánek*, which is the venacular name for buxus sempervirens or common box). If you have a strip of gold leaf then decorate the apple with a golden belt.

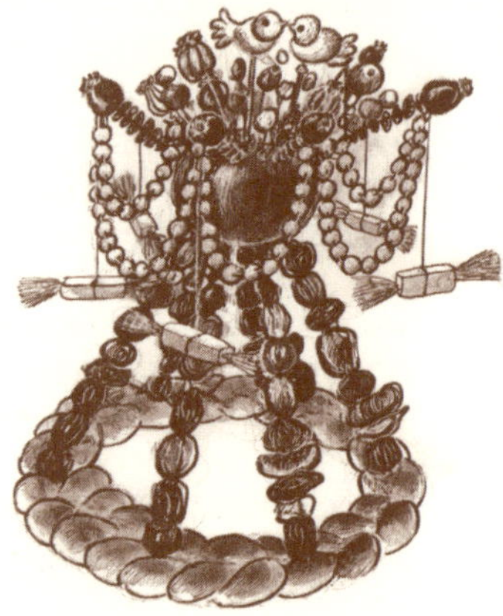

Nicholas plait in a pot (Mikulášský vrkoč v hrníčku)

This nice bushy forest of goodies on sticks in a stout ceramic pot used to be prepared by mums in Eastern Bohemia for their children as a St Nicholas window surprise. We might go back to this tradition, not so much for the sweet treats (nowadays children may well prefer a Kinder Surprise) as for the marvellous colourful and aromatic pot that enhances your home at Advent time.

Stick dried plums, apples, pears, apricots, figs, nuts (which might even be gilded), rosehips, almonds, little birds and pellets baked from yeast dough, poppy heads, little *panenská* apples, snow cookies, little gingerbread figures, swollen peas and raisins onto a large number of approximately 15 cm long skewers. Pour sand or stuff floral foam into a fine stout ceramic pot, preferably of a single colour, and moisten. Then cover the entire surface with a dense little garden of small box twigs. Finally stick in the prepared skewers of little treats to radiate outwards. You can then tie thin red ribbons onto some of the skewers.

Devils, chimney sweeps and ladies made from dried fruit (Čerti, kominíci a dámy ze sušeného ovoce)

The last markets of the year, St Nicholas fairs, sold not only ordinary goods, but also Christmas presents, delicacies, southern fruit, Christmas crèche figures and spices for Christmas cooking. Naturally, most of all the children liked the figures made out of dried fruit, which they could play around with and then simply eat. The body of the devil is made of dried pear, fig and a little red apple or a little yeast-dough scone or gingerbread. The hands, legs and head are made from dried plums on sticks, while

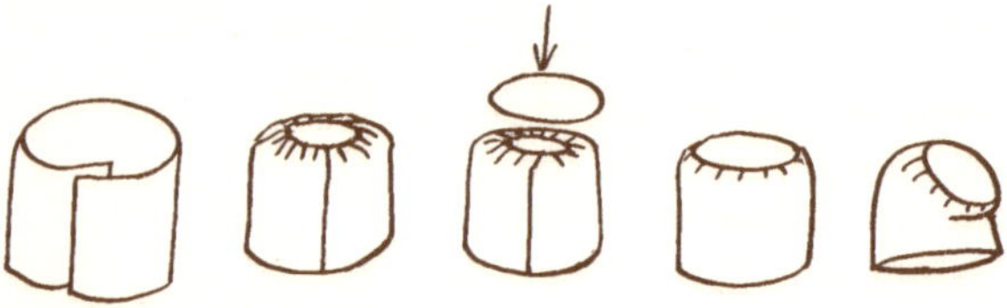

the horns are made from nicely shaped desiccated apple or from little sticks with raisins. For the devil to stand up on his own he needs not only his two legs, but also a third point of support formed by a tail made from wire wrapped round with string and bound at the end with red ribbon. Fray out the remaining string in a tassle. The devil should be holding a fork made out of a skewer and gold foil or a little scourge made of small dry twigs. Make the tongue out of red paper and the eyes out of royal icing (as for gingerbread) or out of white paper wheels with red centres. Fasten a chain of raisins or swollen peas from his arm to his belt made out of a gold foil strip.

A chimney sweep is made in a similar way to a devil, except that the axis of the body, i.e. the head, the trunk and one leg are spiked onto a single stick and the other limbs are stuck onto wire. Glue his cap together from pieces of white canvas or paper, and glue his little ladder together from shortened skewers. Make his chimney-sweep's broom out of wound wire and wind a tuft of black pack thread to the end.

Bake the lady's pedestal out of gingerbread or yeast dough. Stick a central skewer into this and impale figs or large flakes of desiccated apple onto it as her skirt. The torso will be made of sweet chestnut - run it through with a wire the length of your hand and stick dried plums onto it. The head can be made out of a plum, a pellet of baked dough or shredded almond. Make the hat out of a large dried apricot and decorate with a cockade made out of a strip of white paper.

Quiver tree (Třesolka)

An appealing toy and table decoration. Pluck all the down from a large goose quill and chop or cut up its thick bottom end into as many narrow strips as possible. Then impale presoaked swollen peas on their ends and insert the entire little palm tree into a large red apple. The peas at the ends of the quill will keep shivering and quivering - hence the name *třesolka*, or elsewhere *třezolka* - quiver tree. Eventually the peas will dry out and hold firm to the quill ends, and if you carefully insert the quill into the core, an apple of this kind will last for quite a long time.

Candied roasted nuts (Griliáš)

If you want to treat the children and at the same time create a nice table decoration then make some *griliáš*.

Burn several sugar cubes moistened in water in a largish saucepan. Prepare in advance several skewers with various treats - nuts, dried fruit and little almond pellets. When the caramel acquires a golden copper hue, submerge the skewer and its contents in the hot sugar coating, but then immediately dip in ice-cold water. A hard vitreous substance will form on the surface, which is all very fine and striking, though perhaps not all that healthy for your

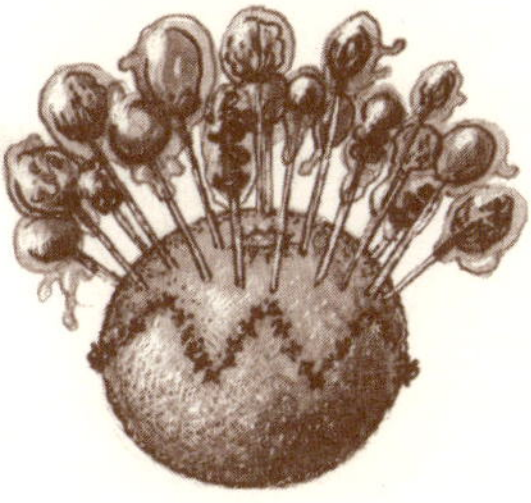

teeth. Then stick the skewers into apples or oranges and you can also decoratively stick cloves in the fruit peel so that they chime – and there you have both an interesting decoration for the Christmas table and a fine treat for the children.

Shaped bread (Tvarované pečivo)

Bread accompanied most important annual festivities in the past. Sourdough bread increases in volume, and so in people's superstitious minds it was meant to ensure acquisition of property and good crops. If one gave the bread the shape of an animal or a magic figure then you augmented this effect. Anybody who received such bread figures as a gift and ate them was meant to obtain not only riches and happiness, but also the qualities that were ascribed to various animals, e.g. the agility of a lizard, the wisdom of a snake, the virile nobility of a stag and the like.

Dough for shaped bread: 500 g plain flour, two tbsps of sugar, half a coffee spoon of salt, three tablespoons of oil, 20 g of yeast (not quite half a cube), one egg, yolk for brushing, lukewarm milk to prepare firm dough.

Mix all the loose ingredients into the flour. You might also add a pinch of turmeric to improve the colour. Then crumble the yeast into the mix, add the egg, oil and a little lukewarm milk. Carefully knead into a firm, smooth dough, like that of home-made noodles. Keep beneath a dish or in a freezer bag. Immediately separate little pieces of dough and shape them. Make the animals' eyes out of black peppercorns, which are to be moistened a little before being wedged into the animals' heads. These shapes are mostly made from strands of dough, decorated by cutting with scissors, pricks and other ornamentation. Place on an oil-brushed tray and leave to rise a little. Then leave to bake in a not too hot oven – the shapes should be baked slowly. After ten minutes of baking brush the bread with whipped egg-yolk and leave to finish baking.

World - king (Svět - král)

Polish a large red apple and plant a little tomato garden in its top half - with poppy heads, rose-hips, raisins, swollen peas, nuts, baked bird-shaped dough, dried fruit (dessicated apple and pear, plums, apricots, raisins and figs) or little gingerbread figures stuck onto short skewers or toothpicks. Some sticks may also be decorated with squares or wheels of pre-starched, ironed gingham (ideally checkered red and white). Finish everything off with box twigs and place the apple decorated in this way on a tripod made of sticks wrapped round with a strip of red paper. Finally, find a little red apple and with red cotton thread round its stalk fasten it like a bell to the stalk of the large apple. And there you have a celestial hanging garden with the poor little world swinging below...

Hedgehog (Ježek)

This counterpart to the "king" from Southern Bohemia is appropriately named after the spines on this little creature. All the skewered items detailed in the previous instructions, the

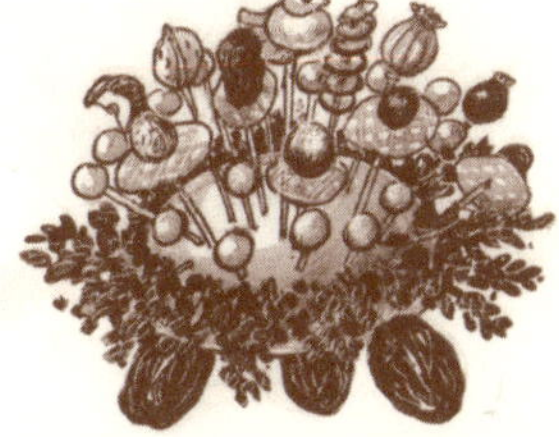

symbols of plenty, fertility, happiness and health, are to be stuck into a little loaf baked out of dough (like the shaped bread). But it can also be Christmas cake dough. Knead a smooth bun in your hand and bake. Leave to cool. It is best to wait till the next day to work with the bread. Sometimes the loaf is placed on a tripod made of prunes on sticks.

Little garden (Zahrádka)

A Christmas folk artifact, which - if you add candles - can work nowadays as a lovely Christmas Eve candle holder. It is a structure made of five red apples interconnected with raisin-impaling skewers. The apples are topped off with green box twigs and perhaps those candles too, although they need to be prepared in advance. Dip them for a while in hot water, which should come up to around two centimetres of the bottom of the candles.

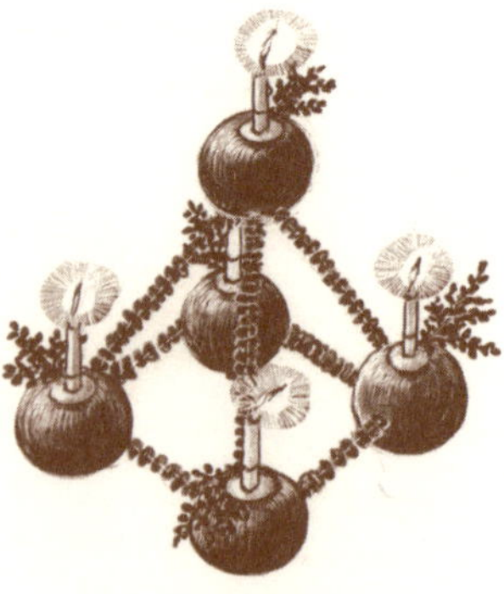

Then you will find it easy to insert the toothpicks into the softened wax or stearin. To prevent any damage to the candle from the water make a cuff from a strip of gold foil. Also stick the foil onto stiff paper, cut out a wheel and make a hole in the middle through which you can insert a toothpick into the candle. The candle prepared in this way can then be stuck into the apple core.

Blackthorn branch (Trnková větev)

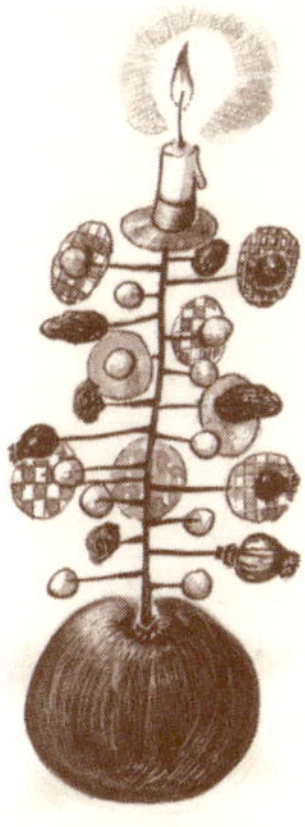

Thorny young blackthorn shoots are rather reminiscent of Christmas trees. In folk mythology the thorny branches had a protective function. Stick smaller young blackthorn shoots that are nice and evenly branched into a large apple at the apple corolla, removing or shortening the stalk beforehand, so that the apple stands up straight. Stick sprouted peas onto the thorns - soak unpeeled green or yellow peas overnight in cold water then pour off the water and put the peas into a freezer bag, so that they do not dry out until you work with them. Other decorations with a similar significance can be stuck on the ends of the thorns besides peas - rosehips, dried fruit, gay folk materials cut into circles or squares or red wheels and golden paper. At the end of the switch stick a gilded nut or a small candle prepared as per previous instructions. A large dramatically branching blackthorn or hawthorn branch (without leaves and fruit) with a large number of peas stuck on the thorns, and occasionally decorated with red and white checked or striped gingham and perhaps several birds baked out of dough can be marvellously decorative. In a largish slim ceramic bottle it stands out against a smooth white wall even in a modern interior.

Sun orb (Polaz)

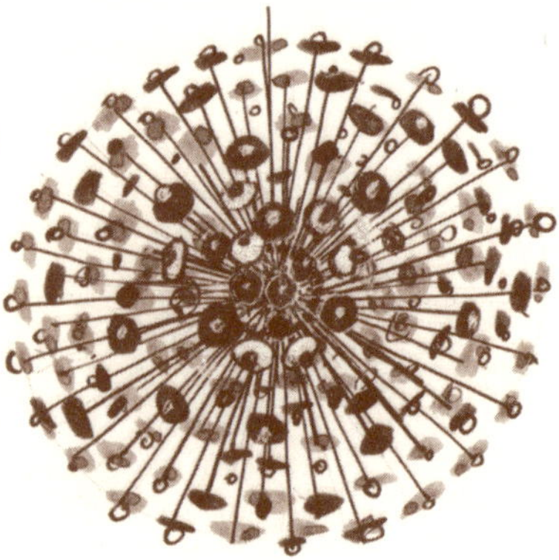

In many Christmas and New Year folk artifacts, the original solstice symbolism can be seen. The basic roundness of the red apple or the golden shining sourdough bread with various symbols of fertility, light, health and plenty radiating out of it – these are actually little suns that help people through times of winter depression, fear and illness. For people in the past the sun was the basis of life, bringing light, warmth and the next harvest. Hence the winter solstice festivities were celebrated with great reverence during pagan times and then in the Middle Ages. It is not by chance that the Christian church grafted the anniversary of the birth of Christ onto the period in which the solstice celebrations came to a head. The Lord's birth date was disputed up until the fourth century – and it was only then that Pope Liberius set December 25th as the definitive date.

One of these sun-shaped ceremonial artifacts is the *polaz* ceiling hanger (evidently from Old Slavonic "*polaziti*" – to go carol-singing). The *polaz* hung in the house lobby and carol singers coming into the house with gifts and good wishes could pick treats off it.

Originally it was an apple or a potato from which numerous wooden splinters offering various treats radiated out. If you try to make a *polaz* today, use modelling clay, a polystyrene ball or a firm ball of moss wound round with thin wire; before sticking the splinters in, moisten their ends in Herkules glue or use a hot melt glue gun. About 150 splinters fit onto a *polaz* and it is quite a laborious affair. But the result is worth the effort and it can be decorative all year round, though for this reason the core should be made of material that does not decay.

Advent wreath (Adventní věnec)

Just like the Christmas tree the Advent wreath is a modern-day tradition. It is so popular these days that I present instructions for a simple little table Advent wreath. Trim off some fine twiglets from several fir twigs and weave a circular base for the wreath from any remaining twigs. Add more twigs to this base and wrap round

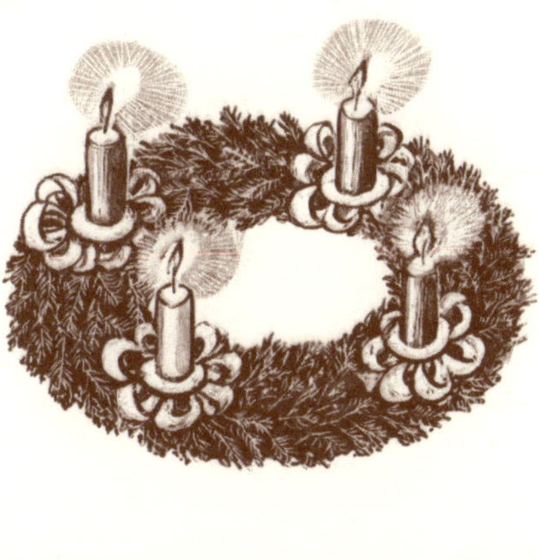

firmly with binding wire. Tie four decorative ribbons into a cross and insert four candles into the fir twigs - in accordance with liturgical convention three of them are to be violet (the colour of fasting) and one of them pink. The candles are lit every Advent Sunday - a new one each week - and the pink one is for the third Sunday, dedicated to Jesus' mother Mary and preparations for the birth of the child, all in a spirit of happiness and expectation.

Christmas Eve wreath with fruit (Štědovečerní věneček s plody)

People used to place everything that was harvested and that they wished to harvest the following year on the Christmas Eve table. Nowadays we can adapt this memory of our forebears and their customs in a mildly stylized form, but without losing sight of the original symbolism and meaning of the objects involved.

Bake a small dough wreath. Prepare all the required components in a little bundle and fix these (stick them or bind them) to a short pointed stick. Then arrange a bunch of ears of grain, flax, dried fruit pinned to sticks, a small apple, onion, garlic, nuts, bread (bird shapes and pellets with peas pinned onto small splinters in them), gingerbread figures, little red ribbons, sprigs of green box and a fine dried mushroom slice by pinning them onto the wreath. You can also add four candles and the wreath then serves as a fine candle holder in the middle of the table, in which case you just have to make sure the candles do not get too close to flammable materials like cereal and flax, or instead of supper you will have to call the fire brigade.

POSTSCRIPT

Our look at the cuisine and all the preparations that went into Christmas Eve and Christmas Day a hundred years ago is drawing to a close. It may inspire many of you and induce many others to think back to, over and about your childhood. I believe that many old recipes are passed down among you from generation to generation in hand-written or loose-leaf cookbooks, so that you already know most of these recipes. It was not my intention to bring a new Christmas recipe cookbook onto the market – it was more my wish to bring some contentment into your homes and hearts. And not only for Christmas. May peace be in your souls all next year and the years to come and in these hurried times of ours may you at least occasionally find little ways to return to the modesty and humility of our forebears.

Happy New Year.

Kamila Skopová

**

Fasting (půst) *- The fast is to be observed throughout Advent, i.e. until the Feast of the Nativity on December 25th. Of course, people used to prepare lots of dishes, pastries, cookies, meat and sauces well in advance, and the hungry maidservant together with the children of the family would nibble at them with great relish beforehand. Hence the superstition that anybody who really fasts honestly to the end of Advent will see a golden piglet, known as zlatoušek, on the wall at suppertime on Christmas Eve. Of course, nobody has ever yet actually seen a golden pig, though people's eyes do flicker when they are very hungry. But above all, the children who used to believe in this were prevented from any premature nibbling - which was evidently the main purpose of the superstition.*

The candles (svíčky) *on the Czech Advent wreath should include three purple ones, symbolizing abstinence and fasting, and a fourth light pink one. The third Sunday of fasting used to be called Silver Sunday in these parts and it is dedicated to the Virgin Mary and the Child, whom she bore under her heart. It was a day full of hope and expectation for the coming event, which differed a little from the otherwise dark and pensive mood of Advent as a whole. Hence its symbolic colour was also pink.*

A Laufr (from German Laufer) *- is a figure that is well-known from the old carnival processions. He led the procession, cracked a whip and asked his hosts' permission for the other masked figures to enter the building. He was gaily dressed in overalls with lots of motley cut-out patches sewn on, which is why people also often called him Ostřížek (Trimming),*

Strakatý (Motley) and Běhoun (Runner), as he quickly ran from building to building, hence Laufr.

***Folk-custom artifacts (zvykoslovné předměty)** - these are objects which for the most part are put together at home for particular requirements, ceremonies, customs and rituals. They always had a certain sense and meaning,*

e.g. as appeals for a good harvest, health, greater possessions and the like. As part of the ceremony involved, these objects were usually destroyed (eaten, burnt etc). Every detail of such folk artifacts had its own symbolism.

***Naggikin and motherkin (klibna a matička)** - the former is a rather stylized mare, similar to those in carnival processions, while the latter is a man dressed up as an old woman to represent the mother of St Nicholas. Hence this little mother played a similar role to that of Nicholas - punishing disobedient children and rewarding the well-behaved.*

***Devil (čert)** - in contrast to the Austrian Krampus and the German Teufel, the Czech devil is quite good-natured, though a little dimwitted and naive. He does no harm to anybody and the children are not very afraid of him.*

***Fortune-telling with apples and walnut-shell boats (věstba z jablka a ořechových loděk)** - a very popular game for divining one's health in the year to come - each person selects an apple and cuts it in half. If the core just shows a little star then everything will be fine, but if the core is in any way unusual or shows a cross, or if the apple is wormy then that is a bad sign. People used to be very superstitious about this. Launching a little* *candle stub in a walnut-shell on water in any largish receptacle is more of a social amusement. The way that the little boat floats along is meant to represent the fate of its owner in the year to come. If the shell floats away from the side of the receptacle, this means you will move away from your parents' home. A candle that quickly goes out indicates sickness or death. An erratically flickering flame symbolizes problems of some kind, while a clear, steady flame means tranquillity, well-being and the like.*

Christmas cake (vánočka) *– this is old-time bakery which demonstrably goes back to the 14th century. It also used to be called "calta", "štědrovka", "houska" and "húsce". It is similar to German and Austrian Stollen, although vánočka is more like a sweet bread with raisins, braided in the form of a layered plait. This plait is freshly baked, not baked several days in advance like the German Stollen.*

Kamila Skopová (1944) – Prague High School of Applied Arts graduate and artist. Apart from her profession she is also engaged in the study of ethnography. She has worked together with a number of folklore groups, creating numerous exhibitions of folk customs and practices, staged sequences, replicas of folk costumes, musical instruments and folk artifacts. She teaches at the School of Folklore Traditions and has published: *Lidová tvorba* (Folk Art) (1995), *...ale máma to vařila líp* (...But Mum Cooked it Better) (2003, 2009), *Rodinné stříbro aneb Klenoty české domácí kuchyně* (Family Silver or Gems of Czech Home Cooking) (2005), *Velikonoční svátky o století zpátky* (Easter a Century Ago) (2007), *Hody, půsty, masopusty* (Feasts, Fasts and Carnivals) (2007), *Dětské hrátky půlstoletí zpátky* (Children's Games Half a Century Ago) (2008), *Rodinné svátky o století zpátky* (Family Festivals a Century Ago) (2010), *Rok na vsi* (The Year in the Village) (2011). She has also illustrated a number of other books. She lives in Oldřetice near Hlinsko.

CONTENTS

Böhmische Weihnachten sind ein Begriff an sich. Was steckt dahinter? Als wir 2004 dieses Büchlein von Kamila Skopová erstmals veröffentlichten, ahnten wir nicht, welche Tradition wir damit begründen würden. Seit damals erscheint die tschechische Originalversion dieses kleinen Buches mit steigender Auflage fast jedes Jahr neu. Wodurch fesselt es das Interesse seiner Leserinnen und Leser? – Diese Publikation von Kamila Skopová (1944), bildende Künstlerin und Volkskundeexpertin, welche in ihrem gezimmerten Häuschen im Hügelland bei Hlinsko in Ostböhmen lebt, bringt die tschechische Weihnachtsatmosphäre vor allem anhand eines Themas in die Gegenwart, welches im Rahmen der weihnachtlichen Traditionen bis heute bei uns am lebendigsten geblieben ist – anhand der Festtagsküche. In ihren spannend geschriebenen Erzählungen darüber, was unsere Vorfahren am Weihnachtstisch servierten, verbunden mit welchen Bräuchen und Traditionen, finden wir auch praktische Weihnachtsrezepte, aktualisiert und an die heute erhältlichen Rohstoffe angepasst. Das Buch wird von feinen Illustrationen der Autorin anschaulich ergänzt. Es ist also kein Wunder, dass die „Böhmischen Weihnachten" ihre schrittweise Fortsetzung in einer Reihe von weiteren Büchern der Autorin fanden, welche die Feiertage und Traditionen zu Ostern, jene im Rahmen der Familie und auch die Welt der Kinderspiele und -freuden zum Inhalt haben.

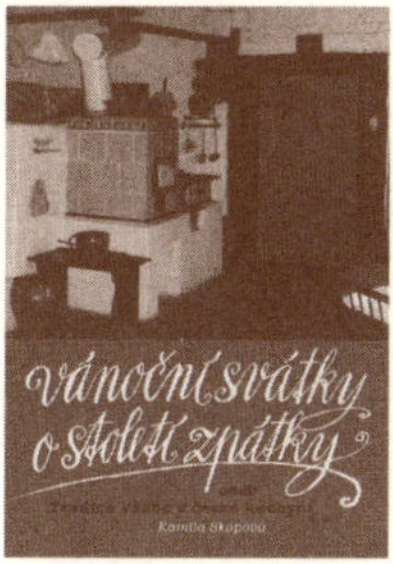

Když jsme obdrželi milý rukopis Kamily Skopové v roce 2004, netušili jsme, jakou tradici vánočních knížek s ním otevíráme. Od té doby vychází tato drobná knížka téměř každoročně ve stále se zvyšujícím nákladu. Čím si Vánoční svátky získaly zájem čtenářů? - Vánoční publikace Kamily Skopové (1944), výtvarnice a folkloristky, žijící v malé roubence na Vysočině u Hlinska, zpřítomňuje atmosféru českých Vánoc skrze téma, jež je v rámci vánočních zvyků dodnes u nás nejživější - tj. téma sváteční kuchyně. V poutavě psaném povídání o tom, co servírovali naši předci na vánoční stůl, s jakými zvyky a tradicemi, najdeme i praktické vánoční recepty, aktualizované na dnešní běžně dostupné suroviny. Knížku doprovází autorka jemnými ilustracemi. Není tedy divu, že na Vánoční svátky navázala postupně celá série autorčiných knížek, mapující svátky a obyčeje velikonoční, rodinné a také svět dětských her a radostí.

Published by Filip Tomáš - Akropolis
(Severozápadní IV 16/433,
141 00 Praha 41, www.akropolis.info)
in 2012 as their 230th publication

English translation Melvyn Clarke
Cover image Blahoslav Lukavec
www.vanocnivystava.cz
Graphic layout Filip Tomáš
Typesetting Ondřej Fučík
Printing Tiskárna Protisk, s. r. o.,
Rudolfovská 617, 370 01 České Budějovice
1st English edition, 80 pages

ISBN 978-80-7470-015-6